BOOKS BY ROD McKUEN

POETRY

AND AUTUMN CAME
STANYAN STREET AND OTHER SORROWS
LISTEN TO THE WARM
LONESOME CITIES
IN SOMEONE'S SHADOW
CAUGHT IN THE QUIET
FIELDS OF WONDER
AND TO EACH SEASON
COME TO ME IN SILENCE
MOMENT TO MOMENT
CELEBRATIONS OF THE HEART
BEYOND THE BOARDWALK
SLEEP WARM

COLLECTED POEMS

TWELVE YEARS OF CHRISTMAS
A MAN ALONE
WITH LOVE . . .
THE CAROLS OF CHRISTMAS
SEASONS IN THE SUN
AN OUTSTRETCHED HAND
ALONE

COLLECTED LYRICS

NEW BALLADS
PASTORALE
THE SONGS OF ROD MCKUEN
GRAND TOUR

CELEBRATIONS OF THE HEART

celebrations of the heart

ROD McKUEN

CHEVAL
BOOKS
—
SIMON AND
SCHUSTER
—
NEW YORK

Published by Simon and Schuster
Rockefeller Center, 630 Fifth Avenue
New York, New York 10020
and
Cheval Books
8440 Santa Monica Blvd.
Los Angeles, California 90069
Manufactured in the United States of America

First printing October 1975

1   2   3   4   5   6   7   8   9   10

Library of Congress Cataloging in Publication Data

McKuen, Rod.
    Celebrations of the heart.

    Poems.
    I. Title.
PS3525.A264C4   811'.5'4   75-25877
ISBN 0-671-22168-X
ISBN 0-671-22169-8 (deluxe)

This collection is for
David Osborne.

CONTENTS

AUTHOR'S NOTE

The major part of this book was written in California and London in the spring of 1975. It was completed that same year on June 21st in Cape Town, South Africa. Some additional material was added in July in Sydney, Australia and again in California.

R.M./1975

CELEBRATIONS

---

to Larry Phillips

Plan One

Celebrations of the heart do not come easy. Yet they abound and sound around us, waiting only for the merrymakers to enter and start the revelry.

Rather than confound a new love with confetti or take one unaware by putting on the kind of mask that puts one off, open up. Let go. The worst you'll come away with is a tin horn blaring in your ear, a firecracker burn, or someone's hastily scribbled address wadded in your pocket.

Piñatas and Christmas crackers abound in celebrations small or large, needing only to be broken open. Go then with a cane and wave it in the air. The festival begins when you are ready—not a moment sooner.

EXCELSIOR

I celebrate your eyes
because they looked at me
without restraint
            and no shame.

I celebrate your breasts
in the darkest night
I could find them blind
            and feeble.

I celebrate your tears
even if they cry for something
            that I've done.

I celebrate you
playing shuffleboard
                or tennis
or playing with my balls
while I sleep.

I celebrate
all the night sounds
that you make
but won't admit to
your conversations with yourself
                in sleep.

Most of all
I celebrate the god
that gave me you
and asked for nothing
              in return.
He'll get a better man
one with more compassion
because he let me
stumble onto you.

SOME SILENT WINTER

How it must feel
to light the world
with bon-bon songs
and never weep again
in the darkness or the noon.

But sweet songs
come from covenants with God,
if you would sing sweetly
be sure the right God
catches you while walking
and when he turns you 'round
be sure he walks you safely
down the first half mile.

And now I love you
and I live you as well
because of you I am larger
                    than myself
I am as big as both of us
I live because I love you
I love because
there is you to live for
and you to love,
and falling asleep against you
or thinking I'm against you
is all the bon-bon song I need
to fill my world.

SOME SILENT SPRING

Some silent spring
when everything is so quiet
only the piper down the field
is making sounds
we'll take the season at its word.
I'll bring you willows
from the wood's edge
we'll sit quietly
waiting for the deer
to come into the clearing
                        for water.

ELDON, ONE

Maybe there are
no more doors
if this is so
I'm glad the last one
opened up on you.
Should I go on ahead
I'll leave a trail
of bread crumbs
or multi-colored twine
to help me find
the way back
to this happy place.

Having seen your eyes
I need no different
shades of green.

AUGUST RAINBOWS

And after every summer rain
an August rainbow
sunlight in the good green wood
laughter in the town
shelter in the noontime shadows
or here inside each other's arms.

No one can kill our rainbows
though sometimes the world
seems bent on trying.

I want you to remember
when things don't go exactly right
in your outside world
that there is safety here.
A rainbow bridge,
a patch of light
at the end of trouble's tunnel.

Walk down the day easy
knowing our security
                    is movable
going wherever we go.

ADMISSION

Crawl with me
     through dawn
starting early.
So that we might do
     everything
there is to do.
Don't be the first
to go to sleep
or if you do
let me fall asleep
     inside you.
Let me hibernate
like a chipmunk
     or a bear
in the middle winter.

ELDON, TWO

Your jealousy
below the colored lights
did not displease me.
Unwarranted or not
it said in silence
     those words
we should not say aloud
        just yet.

You honor me
with your attention,
your jealousy has made me proud.

Most of all
I confess that my existence
only comes from
            loving you.
Were it not so
I don't know
where my head would be.
In the meat rack
or on the chopping block
                I suspect.

ELDON, THREE

Twenty-nine flights up
the wind surrounding us
whistling, pounding
sounding like no wind
          ever sounded.

Safely
we rode out the night
          together.
When the sunlight came
you hid us both
  behind a pillow.

That first night behind us
a week now gone
a new one coming
you hide me still.
I am safe and sleepy
smiling, unafraid
ready to go forward
not walking, running
through all the storms
and all the sunshine
           up ahead.

STARTS AND STOPS

for Lowell Haver

Plan Two

Starts and stops are everything. *They are in themselves a beginning and an end. But more, within them lies the only pleasure life affords. I regret no love affair however small or temporary. I do not blame those who promised fidelity for always, then tired and went away. I rejoice that I have known the company of giants, even for a small time.*

If I have regrets or feel inadequate, it comes from quarrels of my own making. Blindness to apology . . . sonnets made from sincerity that later proved untrue.

I regret that I was not born with a mind as winning as some I've wooed and won.

But I believe that there will always be a second chance, an opportunity for correction.

LETTER FROM SYDNEY

The letter finally came
Bushtail possum
       on the postage stamp
seven days from Sydney
             to L.A.

No six
moving past the dateline
       it came today.

I would that I
were travelling back
with your letter's answer
carried on my tongue
       to yours.

I would look at you
in the easy winter night
of New South Wales
and you would know
that my urgency
for answers to unframed questions
comes from the necessity
of being with you,
not just the luxury or need.
You are a fact for me
        not dream or fiction.

I agree that time
will test us
but time not spent with you
                is lost.

SCRUB PINES

Scrub pines struggle
through the underbrush,
sideways, d
        o
         w
           n,
   up
then   again.
Never really heading skyward
they seem happy to survive
if not really thrive.

Nature never helps
the scrub pine tree,
it seems to caution
get there on your own,
wherever *there* is.
I'm not sure
that even that slow growing
stunted, slanted scrub
could tell you
where it's heading
and which branch
              leads the way.

Scrub pines finally
find their way.
Proud, predictably
          unpredictable
they shoot up through
the underbrush
          and underbelly
of long grass
in their own good time.

Try to help.
Clean and water down
the root,
spread love
to the farthest limb.
It doesn't work.
Their resilience lies
in their own ability
to go and grow alone.

Straighten out
a scrub pine tree
and watch it
snap back in your face
even on a path
you thought familiar
and without peril.

I tried.
But the island,
let alone the world,
is full of stinging faces
        each of whom
can make that statement.

It might have been
                almost enough
if you'd have let me
watch you turn and grow
in your own way
at your own speed.
Even if I'd done my watching
                from an acre off.

But islands never reappear
in quite the same way
as they did at first.
I couldn't find my way
to inlet or to island
          without direction
and certainly
you'd never lead me.

PHANTOM SLEIGH BELLS

There you are and there you go
you didn't and you couldn't
and now you'll never know.

It was you.
It was you.
Why else would I
have looked so longingly.

But never mind
you only helped the sadness
speed a little faster
down the road toward me.

I've learned to live with demons
you could never know.

In a way, it helps
that you didn't understand.

I can look upon you
as the mover of mountains
I could never move
without your knowing,
without having to trouble you.

THE RHYTHM OF SPRING

All the trees are pink.
Plum blossoms,
or are they small extensions
            of the clouds,
fill the lower sky
above the horizon
trapping the season
for all time,
or for what time
        we know it.

Your smile is only your smile
or is it?
Maybe it's one more opening
                into you
that I should come through
                softly

Softly, I will come,
I will be
concerning you.
Your rhythm will be my own.
Even your heartbeat
should not be
        independent.

PENANCE

Tonight
I will do nothing.
Not read or write
        or think.
I will not let
        television's bromide
           pacify me,
nor make long distance calls
or cruise the *local*
or let Jeri Southern
conjure up old loves for me.

I will sit in this room,
not try to sleep,
disregard the animals
unless they come to me
and if the doorbell rings—
           unlikely,
it will go on ringing.

I am doing penance
not feeling sorry for myself
misjudged or misrepresented.
I feel nothing.
So I will do nothing.

Perhaps there is
a slight ache somewhere
but it is so far
back inside of me
that it remains undiagnosed
and will go unattended.

I am not sure
I could say with certainty
what I am doing
            penance for.
The reason
if it once was real
            is grey.

Tonight I will do nothing
and that includes
not expecting
the unexpected.

But if it should come . . .

THE SPANISH HILLS

Summer comes late
in the hill country
    trees and grass
both take their time greening.
Bougainvillaea waits
until the middle of July
to climb the walls
and run along fences.
The Spanish hills are slow
to come awake to summer.

I wish that we had moved more slowly
getting to know one another.
            I wish that we
had taken time to know
the things about each other
that we shouldn't know.

I shouldn't know, for instance,
how your sighs are manufactured
            and maybe you
shouldn't know me well enough to know—
                        never mind.

The sun
is on the Spanish hills
I fear we'll not go
                running there.
Not today or ever.

WATCH FOR THE WIND AND WAIT

Watch for the wind and wait
when you see it, I'll come home
Listen for the sun
and then be anxious
when you hear the sun move
through the cottonwoods
and down the hill
I'll not be far behind.

Stop time if you can
and if you can't
you'll prevent my leaving.

It's not that I've packed
all my bags
it's just that my mind
is no longer
like an unmade bed.
It only needs
some making over.

When will I be back?
Watch for the wind
and wait.

STOP

What is the next hour
worth to you?

What about the days to come?
Is that hour
and are those days
worth all the young men
in the streets
and parks
that being here with me
will make you miss?

Count carefully.

STARGAZING

to Melanie Millin

Plan Three

Walk out into the darkness and look up. What you see is not a single star but many. Too few to fill so vast a sky but more than enough for God to jingle in his pockets.

Looking at stars becomes for some an avocation (a simple step to rhyme that word with emulation). But if you stargaze long enough you learn that no two fire balls or constellations are alike. And the star that shines the brightest is the one most different. Conclusion: Resolve to be more different and unique. No. Be unique by being you. No one else can lay claim to your smile or the odd assorted ticks and twitches that jerk the muscles of your brain and body.

STARGAZING

I'm floating
spread-eagled
held down by stars.
I want to believe you
because I want you
and so I believe
I do.

But what a wonder
you
close on me and caring
saying that you care.
Stay
I'm coming over there.
Better
best.

I am floating
spread-eagled
lifted up by stars.

JUNE FLIGHT

Airborne—free—
running with the sun
diving down the day
jumping through June—

Above the world
part of the shell
of some new world.

Now end over end
dipping with the down-draft.

Hold onto me—I'm falling
catch me—if I do
never like this,
never like this.

BERTHA'S PLACE

Come on in—
if you're a friend of Bertha's.

I am never sure anymore
if they are cruising me
or recognizing me.

Once a girl said
I remember you
you used to play
in them Roy Rogers movies.

I am not who you think I am
I replied
My name is Truman Capote
and I was once President
of these United States
Of course, I should have said
Let's go home—I'll be who you want.

But I'm only brilliant
when the chance has passed.

for D.J.

VOCAL LESSONS

You want to sing
I could make it so.
But would you
            sing for me?

Not for my ears only,
but for my dissemination
to this world
and all the others.
Only after every note
was hummed and honed
to perfect pitch.

Each cadenza
ascended like a staircase
me watching all those notes
forming in your chest
heaving upward
like a too-long suppressed sigh
until they reached
                and finally escaped
your so loved mouth.

Oh, I could be a teacher
better than the best.
I'd have you singing
with your arms and legs
and all your body.
Your back no less
                than your full voice.

Every sparrow
once he's learned
              to serenade,
leaves the nest
and soars out on his own
                      to fly.

I ask no security
no contract from you,
only that you let me
give to you
              another life.

Using just
the raw ingredients
of your sweet voice
and a little time,
I'd have you singing
softer than the mother hen
                    at mealtime
louder than the radio
            inside the wall.

Hopefully long after
you had flown your cage
some trust in me
would still remain,
Even if the need was gone
I'd take my chances
          on the trust.

Did I read
in small print somewhere
in brief but pointed
          program notes
that you want to sing?
I accept the challenge.
When do we begin?

ROOMS

Plan Four

It rained today. All day. Everything was the sound of rain. Children laughing in the streets, police whistles, cars splashing mud at one another —even the music on the radio sounded like the rain.

Tonight the storm's fatigued enough to stop. Or it's resting only long enough to catch a second breath. Earlier I walked down past the railway station. Sometimes on rainy nights I forget I'm in a foreign country.

It's about twelve-thirty now, nearly everybody's gone to bed. The rain's a barrier. A good excuse for going out, a better one for staying home.

How odd it is that we need make excuses to ourselves for odd behavior, like staying home and in one room. Or walking straight ahead into the storm's most inner eye.

Often I think rooms are the only safe places left. Garret rooms, changing rooms and bedrooms as opposed to ballrooms and waiting rooms and auditoriums. Rooms to climb into, change in and finally rooms where sleep comes easy. A room within a room would be the safest place of all. An interior hiding place where only those with proper maps and charts could find you.

Loving sunshine, I have lately been as satisfied beneath skylights as I have beneath stars. Only the rain worries me. I worry that it won't come. I worry that it will.

I am not a rainmaker. For shaping rain or making it, I have no plan. But I promise you that silent rooms are much preferred to those that jog and jostle you to boredom and to death.

ROOM

Ceiling cracks,
    dusty woodwork,
a spider's web half started,
I know this room by heart.
I find my way
from bed to toilet
in the middle of
    the darkest night.

Half asleep or wide awake
I need no map
to help me thread my way
past and in between
the obstacles that fill up full
    this empty room.

I'd post a letter
but I don't know
        your address.
I'd call
but how would I begin
let alone maintain
        a conversation?
Once I'd promised
to forget you
I ran backward
        making sure
that I'd remember you
for always.

The doorbell buzzes
at odd times
in the morning
          or the night,
maybe all day long
if I were here
   to hear it.

I never answer,
since it isn't you.
And if it were
on opening the door
I'd only open
brand new memories
that even as they happened
I'd be making resolutions
          to forget.

FRAGMENT

His arms were every bit
as wide as Texas
and when he spread them
even in a gesture,
I could only picture
how they wrapped you up at night
delivering you across those wilds
                and those divides
that I could never enter
or cross over to on foot
            or even horseback.

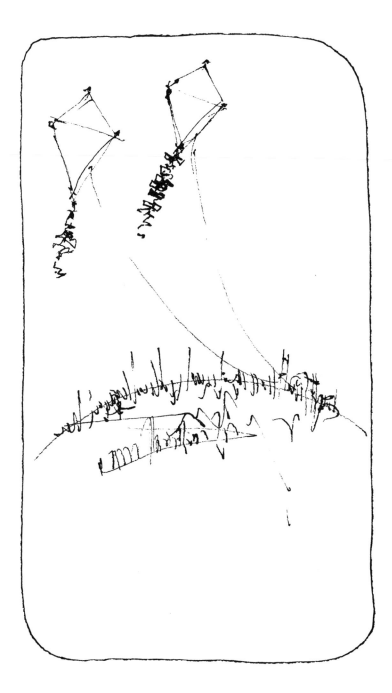

THE HUNTED HUNDRED

Plan Five

*We are the hunters, not the hunted. In the bars
or on the jousting field, we are the seekers.*

*Not lost, we are only between findings. Looking
up from silence into noon and noise. Staring past
tomorrow. Willing we are to try any new way if
it will lead us from the old.*

AUTUMN IS THE MOTHER CHURCH

Always in autumn the hunted hundred
moving separately from the circle
going off into the world
always in autumn.

I kneel before the night
my mother church
and taking its round face into my hands
I pull it to me.

I've learned to take each night
as a new found love,
each autumn night
is now my friend for keeps
my mother church.

THE EYE INSIDE ME

The "I" inside me
asks a single question
one that starts out "Why?"
I can't remember how
to finish off the sentence.

The tomcat I call Tom
goes by eying me.
What does that intelligent animal
of grace and independence see?
Does he see dawns so perfect
that I may never know them,
evenings ending not in struggle
but in peace
even alone, in peace?

God, I am so hungry
I need to eat and drink
        love to last
I wouldn't ask that much
I need a week
a half week
a day
some little time shared
some time not left alone.
I need to wrap my limbs around
a trunk that's strong
but one that melts beneath me.
I pray this autumn won't overtake me
here alone
and that I might finish off
the question that starts out "Why?"

You've known me to be truthful sometimes
believe me now.

I ROLL BETTER WITH THE NIGHT

Wresting with the morning
I come out the loser
lying on the mat
looking up between the thighs of today.
I imagine myself
being picked up
      held, not let go.
Friendly hands
slipped into my back pockets
holding me close against new shoulders
then across my back
hands becoming arms
keep on holding me.

I roll better with the night.
I come up easy in the night
falling back
only when I'm tired and happy.

I don't mean to be indelicate
but I'm always amazed
on meeting someone,
later mouthing them all over
all night long,
then in the morning they leave
afraid to use my toothbrush.

My mouth's now been in and out of yours
and in and out of you so much
that scrubbing down with your toothbrush
is like eating cool mint jelly beans.

It's seven a.m.
another twenty minutes
and we'll both be late.
I don't want to move
and, anyway, my arm's asleep.

I know, I know.
Go, if you like,
but brush your teeth first
on the way to work
you might meet someone
you'd like to smell especially sweet for.

I BELIEVE IN ONE TO ONE

To those few who know me
my religion is well known.
I believe in bodies
        arms entangling
                and untangling.
I believe, and I know it to be so
that there are so many curves
                and hollows
in a single body
        that none of us
none of us
can come to know them all
within a lifetime
but I'll go on trying.

My faith is sure.
It can't be killed or stopped
by one opening I wanted
that didn't open,
by one mound
        that wasn't soft enough
to ease my head,
by one I sought
but didn't win,
by a wound of love
so fresh it hasn't healed.

I believe in one to one
and one on one.
No wine or magic
no hand-me-down Bible
can improve on that.

I believe in spring
but only if I'm rolling in a pillow
or hold some well loved face
is any world green enough for me.

for C.G.

INITIATION

I am ready
white skinned still
not yet stolen by the summer
                          or by anyone.

I am ready, even eager
for the initiation.

I don't know
what I should expect—
freedom from myself?
But I have not felt bound.
A dimension added.
But what is lacking?

I've seen the shadow people
                    gathering
talking of their runs and rallies
but I have never
            gone with them,
always hanging on the fringe.

The major and the minor keys
have intrigued me, yes.
As those that dangle do
but I have been content
to move within the music
                    that I made
playing only those passages
I was sure of
on instruments that needed
                    little amplification.

The rings
were only
rings of sound
that shattered
and then joined
            the silence.

I have been curious
but never this close.
There was no need
to know or to experiment
without instruction.

I know you won't believe me
but I have never known
what it was like
wearing the ring all day
then dealing with the swelling
                              at night.

Whatever toys I've had
were broken by myself
not meant as instruments
                    for the breaking.

I am ready
for *your* way.

Help me
with the breakthrough
so that the initiation
        can be over.

It's very cold in here.

BELCHER LANDING

Plan Six

The war is over now or just beginning. Peace, however hard an interval to make do with, will have to be made do with. I am speaking here of inner wars, childhood meeting age, despair overtaking hope, hope vanquishing despair. The no-man's-land between what we see and what we think we see, that must be crossed.

For me the war is over, this week. I have stopped the pendulum of thought that swings so widely and made it come to rest on but a single subject. Going back. A final, thoughtful look at that terrain and those last outposts of my not so filled up childhood.

The earth is not our dwelling place, *we're meant to rattle here suspended. All the while birth watches us till dying. Some of us cheat death by living out our childhood twice, three, four times over.*

I cannot remember ever having been a sapling. Nor am I yet a tree. When I was younger I was older and now I'm more a child than I should be. Still as I observe my friends and those men not so friendly I find the ones I trust and do believe have a Belcher Landing *of their own that they retreat/return to. It may be a lean-to cabin lived in age of nine, a dog at Christmas, half eleven. Kane's rosebud sled, Jim Kirkwood's pony. A swing within a field within a young girl's mind only. A swing within a summer that was or wasn't but returns and is.*

The mind should have a safe place it can go to ramble. Yours might be in St. Johns Wood or Blissville, Indiana. I have a friend whose mind vacation is nearly always spent barefoot in Tyler, Texas, another half his age who still plays bells in Sgt. Pepper's Lonely Hearts Club Band.

You can go home again, despite your Thomas Wolfe. Never do so on the train, but on the train of thought.

BELCHER LANDING

These days I own
the whole wide ocean—
all the sea
that I can see and more.
Some people say
they're my friends.
It is not enough,
or at the very least too much.

There was a time
sometime ago
when I owned only one small pond
or part of it—
the other part belonged
to my one friend Don.

We'd go swimming at Belcher Landing
Don and me.
Then through the grove
of cottonwoods
still bare-assed and hungry
we'd hunt wild berries
and fall among the fern
no longer wanting
letting the sun get on
with ripening us.
We grew
almost before each others eyes.

Ponds and people grow apart,
new needs push us in new directions
or in no sure direction.

I own the ocean now—
but it is only one small ocean
compared to that one large pond.
Some time ago it was
at the start of one certain summer.
I wonder what became of Don,
Belcher Landing,
and I wonder what became of me?

SUNSET COLORS, ONE

I love the sunset colors
not just in spring but every day.
Every day that God is good enough
to share his red and orange and yellow
with me
      and mine.

Lately I sleep late
and so I seldom see the scarlet morning
or the gold behind the trees.
I depend a lot on sunsets
Even when no sunset comes
I fill my head with all the sunshine past
and sunsets that I know will come.

Looking in your eyes
I see the sun come
even in the darkness.

Do you know how much I feel for you
and in what kind of way?
            I feel the world for you
and in every kind of way.
I think sometimes that I'll explode
that I'll die or disappear
before I have the chance
to tell you how I feel.

Don't let it be today.

SUNSET COLORS, TWO

I'll race you up the hill
we can be children
if we want to be.

It's spring
and there's a difference
between children's games and
                              games.

Besides
we're not so old
we can't be mystified by marigolds
or dazzled by dandelions

Hurry up
grab my hand
        be careful
but not with me.
Why am I running so fast?
to get there soonest.

Like I told you once
I get high on sunshine.

Take that anyway you like.

DARLINGTON POEM

I love you enough
to let you run
but far too much
to let you fly.
Even if you rode home
          on a rainbow
until you reappeared
there'd always be
the chance that you
might not come riding
          home at all.

AND THE HORSE GOES HOME

Rabbits run
geese fly north/south
then homeward, north again.
Every animal or bird
        however small
each thing
that moves beneath
God's benevolent eye
does so only
in God's own good time.

Riding in the field
        this morning;
thinking not about
the needs of all men
but selfishly
of my own needs only
I wondered
as I now am wondering
what design
or brand new plan
God might have in mind
        for me.

Nothing stirs now
no revolution
    has come about
no direction
has changed for me
but I feel
and have been feeling
the need to move.

When the horse beneath me
begins to stomp and chomp
and gallop through the earth
I often wish that it was
my own muscled flesh
thundering through the field
and up the hillsides
sure of where I headed
or positive
        that whatever hand
that guided me, knew.

After the ride,
after all the rides
we head home slowly
        the horse and me.

Not tired but resigned.

ADDENDUM

for Aram Saroyan

Plan Seven

Move ahead.

REPORT ON A LIFE IN PROGRESS
FEB. 1973

I'd rather be
a poet read
than one who postures
for posterity.
As I would rather *love*
and know that I am unloved
than be desired at a distance,
unmoved and unaware.
Having achieved as far I know
these two distinctions
the first has given me
happiness of some measure.
The second one has made me
         not as sad
as some among you might believe.

PREJUDICE

Prejudice is sensible.
Avoid time wasters
and the village gossip.
Give in to all the dislikes
you might harbor
for people on the inside
who would tear down
                any closeness
and confidence
you might have built
or manufactured
for those you love
or those that you
would have love you.

Learn to hate all wars
      holy or otherwise
all those who take shelter
in hating cultures and colors
instead of individuals.

Black isn't always
                  beautiful
but any man who finds it
      wholly ugly
should be shown
the other side of white.

The Jew
who loves the gentile
shouldn't do so
    out of tolerance
only out of love
if that love
    is given back.

Otherwise
love, like jerking off
or playing solitaire
is nearly always
    a waste of time.

Me?
Some of my best friends
are my friends.

THE MUD KIDS

Out of the curious
　　　　foraging rain
moving over the lawn
　　　　like evening,
one by one they come,
the mud kids.

Carrying their mud
　　　　in buckets
sometimes hardened
　　　　into bricks
or molded into
Ken and Barbie dolls.

The ones who claim
we never understand them.

We blame it all
on Freud or Dr. Spock,
a Madison Avenue
cult of youth,
the decline
of moral standards
Urban renewal
Dylan songs
that taught them
        how to think.

Anything but what it is,
the turning from homes
that weren't quite right
and getting up
        from T.V. dinners
to eat the snow,
the playing
with each other
instead of dolls.

Anyway,
who wants to play
with Ken and Barbie dolls
when there's G.I. Joe
with seven different uniforms
acting out their fantasies
nightly on T.V.

Let the mud kids
make their mud pies
and throw them
          at the world.

With their help
it could be
a better place
to live in.
Besides,
     Mack Sennett would be proud.

HILL POEM

Too long
we've looked
for men to match
our mountains,
another way perhaps
of keeping our eyes
always on the core
and not the apple.

Now that men
of seeming sensibility
have all but pulled down
every worthwhile hill
our priorities should be
                    turned around.

Think how it would be,
in California
let alone the world
to find enough new,
or even reconstructed
                    mountains
to match those many men
who level knolls
        and pull down ridges
on unsettled stomachs
                or one whim
by signing just their names
        in triplicate.

for Rebecca Greer

POSITION

I live in America
neither right or left am I
and certainly not center.
To me to be among
the silent majority
means to be among the dead.
And for me
no two or ten or two hundred
make up a minority.
Every man is such
because every man is different.

If I met a man
who looked like me
and thought like me
and walked and spoke like me
and was in no way
different from me
only then would I consider slaying him
for he would have stolen from me
all those truths
and all those lies
I'd found out for myself.

All the living
that had brought me here
that man would have erased
by being just like me.

But kill a man unlike myself?
            Not likely.
There might be something
I could learn from him.

There is so much I need to know,
why there are no butterflies
in the world's backyard,
and when I find out
I need to study
how to get them back.

Men trample beauty underfoot
like it was gravel.
These actions are confined
to no one country
but I resent it in my own
because I love my country.

Could it be
that men join clubs
as men carry them,
        for security?
But from what?

My security is my country
and everything I am in life
and everything I know
and everything I care about
revolves around it.

And I live in America
and I find its face not ugly
except sometimes.

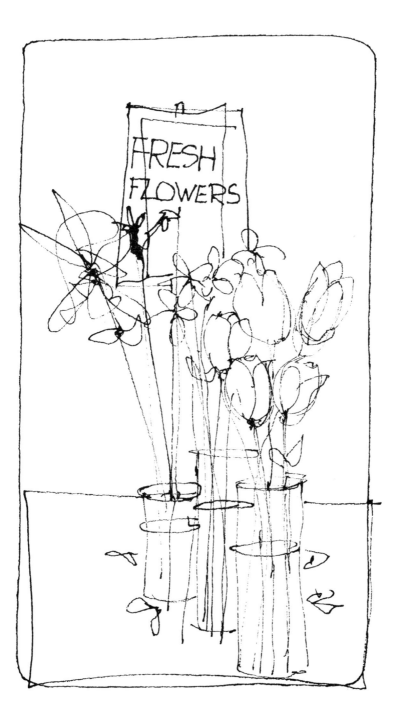

THEY NUMBER FOUR

for Jean Simmons

Plan Eight

Pull the covers closer. Add another blanket if you need to. Winter can't be trusted. And yet your policy should be: In everything I trust.

afterthought, one

Now the memory blurs.
You didn't feed it.
Not to worry,
not to worry.
I'll keep filling in
the holes until they're whole.

afterthought, two

Come then strangers
and those of you I know,
form as one.
I fear you've done so
anyway and already.

And if your name
be litany or lie
I'll love you all the same
if you'll come close enough
to let me.

afterthought, three

Maybe all the promises
            don't come true
but whoever said they did?

The day came, didn't it?
Give me a little more time
give us a little while longer.

Look, there are sparrows on the lawn.

afterthought, four

I'm tired
you'll have to wage
             the revolution
by yourself.

Try not to make
too much noise.

The cat's asleep.

ABOUT THE AUTHOR

ROD McKUEN *was born in Oakland, California, and has traveled extensively throughout the world both as a concert artist and a writer. In just over six years seven of his books of poetry have sold in excess of ten million copies in hardcover, making him the best-selling and most widely read poet of all times. In addition he is the best-selling living author writing in any hardcover medium today. His poetry is taught and studied in schools, colleges, universities and seminaries throughout the world, and the author spends a good deal of his time visiting and lecturing on campus.*

Mr. McKuen is the composer of more than fifteen hundred songs that have been translated into Spanish, French, Dutch, German, Russian, Japanese, Czechoslovakian, Chinese, Norwegian, Afrikaans and Italian, among other languages. They account for the sale of more than one hundred fifty million records. In 1975 he was the first major artist who insisted on performing concerts before multiracial audiences, and was allowed by the South African Government to do so.

His film music has twice been nominated for Motion Picture Academy Awards. Rod McKuen's

143

classical music, including symphonies, concertos, piano sonatas and his very popular Adagio for Harp & Strings, is performed by leading orchestras in the United States and throughout Europe. In May 1972, the Royal Philharmonic Orchestra in London premiered his Concerto No. 3 For Piano & Orchestra, and an orchestral suite, The Plains of My Country. In 1973, the Louisville Orchestra commissioned Mr. McKuen to compose a suite for orchestra and narrator, entitled The City. It was premiered in Louisville and Danville, Kentucky, in October 1973, and was subsequently nominated for a Pulitzer Prize in Music.

Among his newest commissions is a multimedia ballet, requested by Nicholas Petrov, director of the Pittsburgh Ballet, to commemorate the American Bicentennial. It will have its premiere in that city in 1976. His Symphony No. 3, commissioned by the Menninger Foundation in honor of their fiftieth anniversary, has just been premiered in Topeka, Kansas.

Before becoming a best-selling author and composer, Mr. McKuen worked as a laborer, radio disc jockey and newspaper columnist. The author spent two years in the Army, during and after the Korean War.

Rod McKuen makes his home in California in a rambling Spanish house, which he shares with a menagerie of old English sheep dogs and a dozen cats. He likes outdoor sports and driving, and has recently started taking flying lessons. As a balloonist he has flown with his pilot, Ray Gallagher, in the skies above Perris and Beverly Hills, California, Johannesburg, Durban and Cape Town, South Africa, and Indianola, Iowa, among other exotic places.